Paws, Wings, and Hooves

Mammals on the Move

by Keiko Yamashita
photographs by Isamu Sekido

Lerner Publications Company • Minneapolis

*The paw on page 1
belongs to this polar bear.
To find out how bears use
their paws, turn to page 12.*

Series Editor: Susan Breckner Rose

This edition first published 1993
by Lerner Publications Company.
Originally published 1986 in Japanese under the title
Doubutsu No Te by Kaisei-Sha Publishing Co., Ltd.

English translation rights arranged with Kaisei-Sha
Publishing Co., Ltd. through Japan Foreign-Rights Centre.

Library of Congress Cataloging-in-Publication Data

Yamashita, Keiko, 1949-
    [Dōbutsu no te. English]
    Paws, wings, and hooves : mammals on the move /
by Keiko Yamashita; photos by Isamu Sekido.
        p.   cm.
    Summary: Explains how different kinds of feet help
different animals travel from one place to another.
        ISBN 0-8225-2901-7
    1. Animal locomotion–Juvenile literature. [1. Animal
locomotion.] I. Sekido, Isamu, 1946-   ill. II. Title.
QP301.Y3613   1993
599'.01852–dc20   92-18506
                                                      CIP
                                                      AC

Manufactured in the United States of America

1 2 3 4 5 6 98 97 96 95 94 93

Mammals are animals that **nurse**, or feed their young with their milk. Mammals also have fur or hair.

All mammals need to move from one place to another. They move to find food. They move to get away from their enemies. When they are young, they move to stay with their mothers.

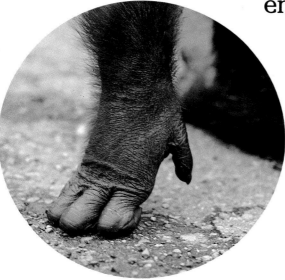

Mammals use their hands, feet, paws, hooves, flippers, or wings to help them move from one place to another. As you read this book, can you figure out how each mammal moves? ▶

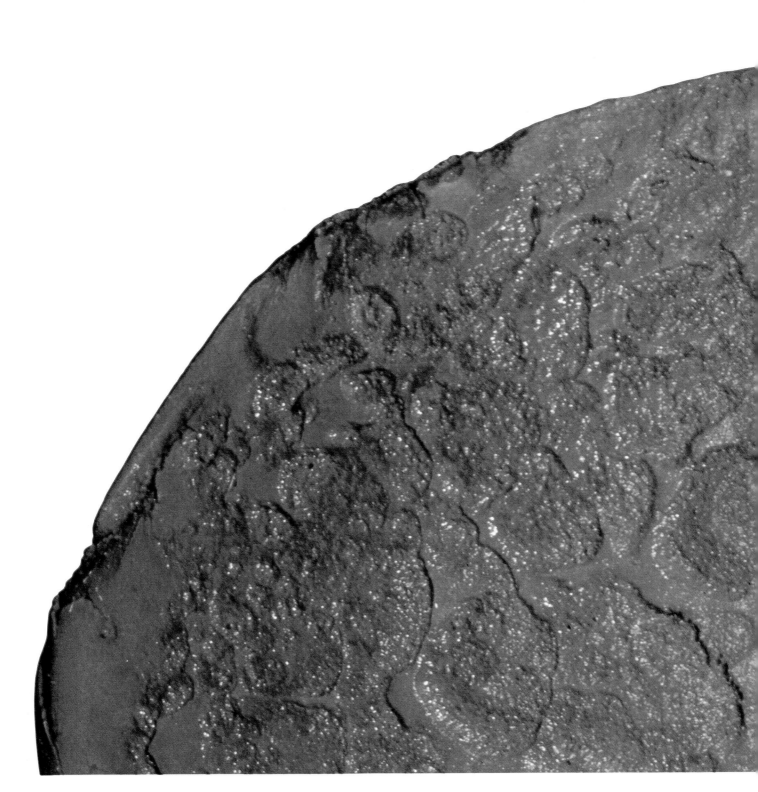

This looks like the surface of the moon, but it is the bottom of a large mammal's foot. This is its actual size.

Which mammal do you think walks on this large, round, heavy foot? ▶

ELEPHANT

African elephants live on the grassy plains, or **savannas**, of central Africa. They walk great distances on their sturdy feet in search of water, and they spend a lot of time standing in muddy river beds.

An elephant's toe bones are hidden inside a thick pad of fat and muscle. This pad acts like a cushion. When an elephant puts its weight on a foot, the pad gets bigger. When the animal lifts its foot up, the pad gets smaller. An elephant may sink deep into mud, but it can easily pull its legs out because its feet become smaller when lifted. The bottom, or **sole**, of each elephant's foot has a spotted pattern different from those of other elephants. ■

Both of these feet are hooves. A hoof is made of a hard substance called **keratin**. Fingernails and claws are also made of keratin. The keratin in a hoof surrounds the toe bones. Hooves are thick and hard and protect the mammal's feet. Whose feet need these hard hooves for protection? ▶

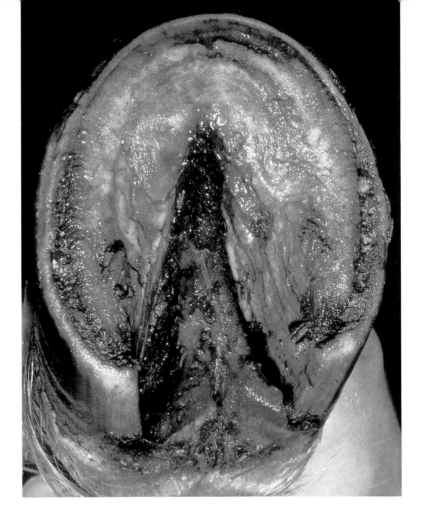

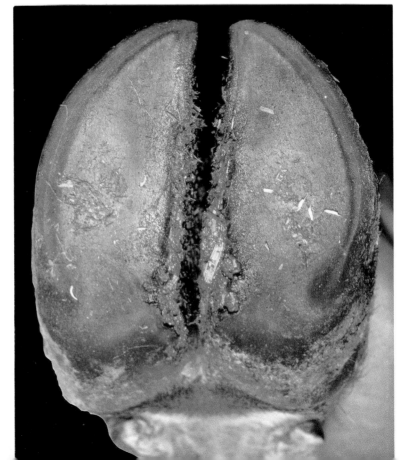

HORSE

Horses' feet are good for running. Each foot is really a strong toe. Only the tip of the toe, protected by the strong, curved hoof, touches the ground. When a horse is galloping, it has only one hoof on the ground at a time.

COW

On hills that are too steep or too rocky to plant wheat or corn, cows eat the grasses. Cows have divided, or cleft, hooves. **Cleft hooves** give cows firm footing on steep or rocky ground. Hooves protect their feet from sharp stones. ■

This foot has three toes. Each toe ends in a separate hoof. The hooves have ridges that look like large, hardened fingerprints. Who walks on this three-hoofed foot? ▶

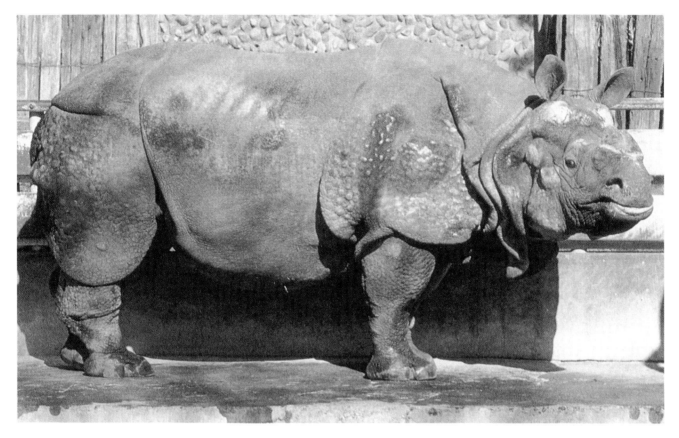

RHINOCEROS

Indian rhinoceroses live in swampy grassland. They spend a lot of time lying in water holes, cooling themselves in the water or rolling in the mud to keep insects away. The ridges on a rhino's hooves keep it from slipping on the muddy banks of the water holes. A rhino's short, stout legs help support its heavy body. Like its hooves, the horn on a rhino's nose is made of keratin. This rhino lives in a zoo, so its horn has been filed down. ■

This paw has five toes that end in long, sharp claws. It belongs to a large mammal that is covered with thick, shaggy fur. Who has this furry front paw? ▶

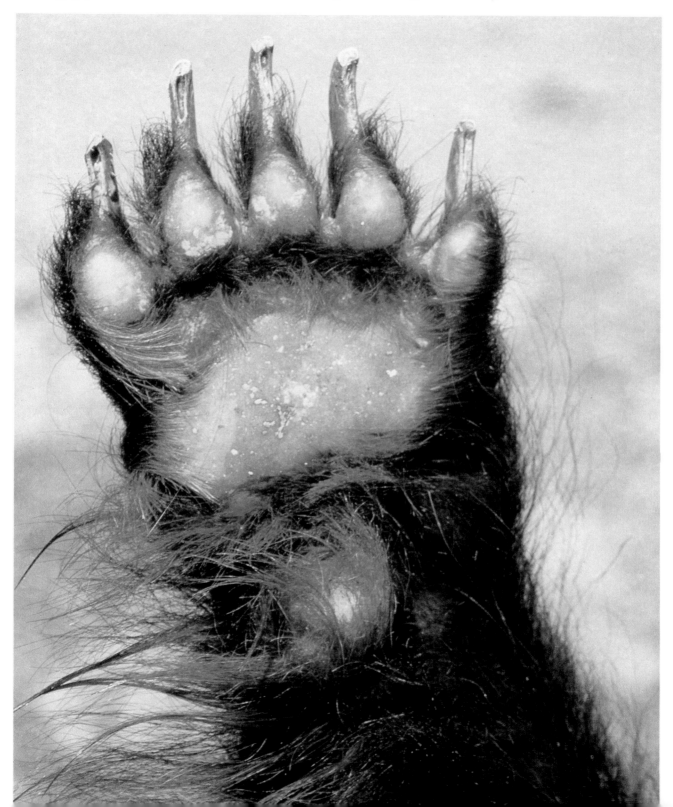

BEAR

Brown bears live in the northern parts of North America, Europe, and Asia, where the winters are long and cold. With the help of their long, sharp claws, bears catch fish in cold rivers. They also dig up roots and small animals that burrow underground. This bear lives in a zoo, and so its claws have been clipped.

Unlike most animals who walk on their toes, bears walk on the soles of their feet. They can even walk upright like a person. ■

This wide, flat front paw with long claws belongs to a small mammal. The mammal stands on its hind paws and digs through the earth with its shovel-like front paws. Who has these paws that dig so well? ▶

MOLE

Eastern moles, like all moles, rely a great deal on touch. Moles are nearly blind. Five sharp claws on each front paw help a mole break up the soil. Then its wide **palms** help it shovel handfuls of dirt aside. A mole's front paws are turned outward, like a pair of oars on a rowboat.

Moles dig tunnels through the earth. Every so often, they dig tunnels up to the surface. These tunnels are called molehills. Moles eat the animals–earthworms, beetles, and slugs–that fall into their tunnels. ∎

Both of these paws belong to mammals who walk on their toes. This helps them run quickly. Spongy pads of thick skin cover and protect the bottom of these paws. The pads also help the animals move quietly. Who can run quickly and quietly on these paws? ▶

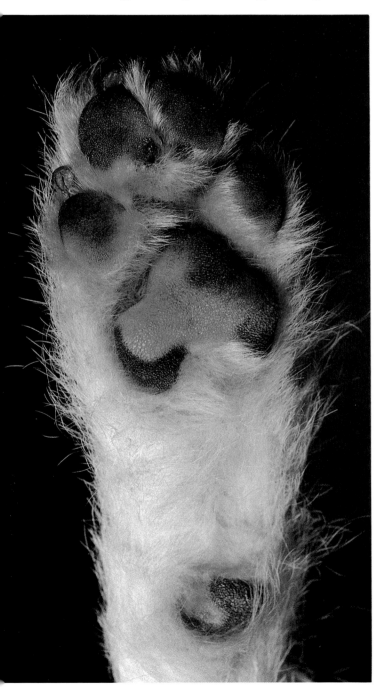
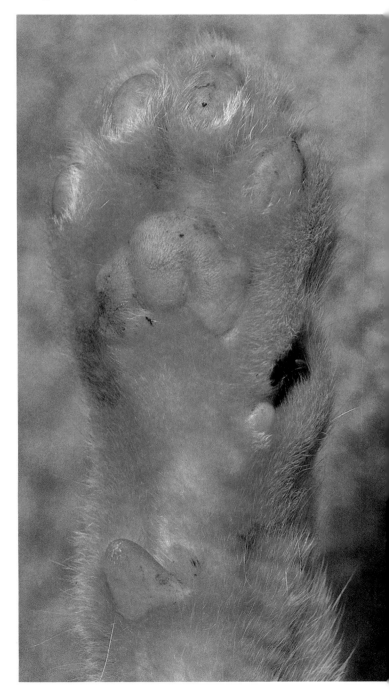

DOG

Dogs are **carnivores**, which means they can hunt and kill other animals for their food. In the wild, many dogs hunt together to surround and catch other animals. Dogs have four toes that end in claws on each foot, and sometimes a fifth toe, or **dewclaw**. The dewclaw does not touch the ground and has no use. This dog's paw does not have a dewclaw, but the cat's paw does. Can you see the cat's dewclaw on page 15?

CAT

Cats are also carnivores. Using their quiet, padded paws, they sneak up on mice and birds. Cats also use their paws to help them find out about the world around them. They bat at things to find out what they are. Cats can keep their claws hidden. Claws that can be hidden are called **retractile claws**. ■

This front paw is a flipper. It belongs to a mammal who spends most of its time in the water. Who swims with this flipper? ▶

SEAL

Harbor seals are powerful swimmers. A harbor seal swims by moving its body and rear flippers back and forth. When a seal is swimming, it uses its front flippers only for steering.

Front flippers also help seals scramble up onto ice or land. Each front flipper has five **webbed** fingers with long, sharp claws. The claws help seals scratch holes into ice. Once on land, a harbor seal uses its flippers very little. It crawls on its belly, humping along like an inchworm by flexing its body. ∎

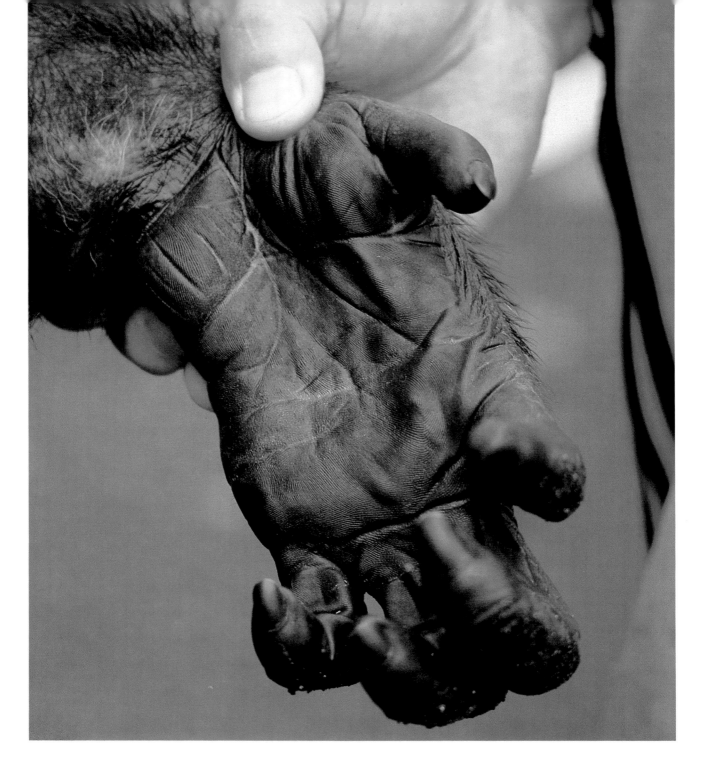

Like a person's hand, this hand has **opposable thumbs**. An opposable thumb can move separately from the fingers on the same hand. Opposable thumbs allow a hand to encircle, or grasp, something. Who grasps things with this hand? ▶

19

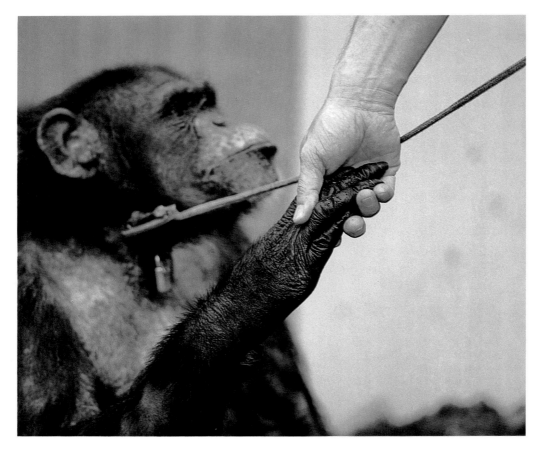

CHIMPANZEE

A chimpanzee's hands can easily grasp and hold onto branches. They have long, muscular fingers. Chimpanzees also have opposable big toes that face sideways like thumbs.

Like people, chimpanzees make tools. For example, a chimpanzee may strip leaves off a twig and poke the twig into a termite hill to catch termites.

Chimpanzees usually walk on their feet and their knuckles. When one chimpanzee greets another, they touch or hug each other. Chimpanzees spend a few hours each day grooming each other. They sit and pick through each other's hair, removing any insects, leaves, or dirt that they might find. ■

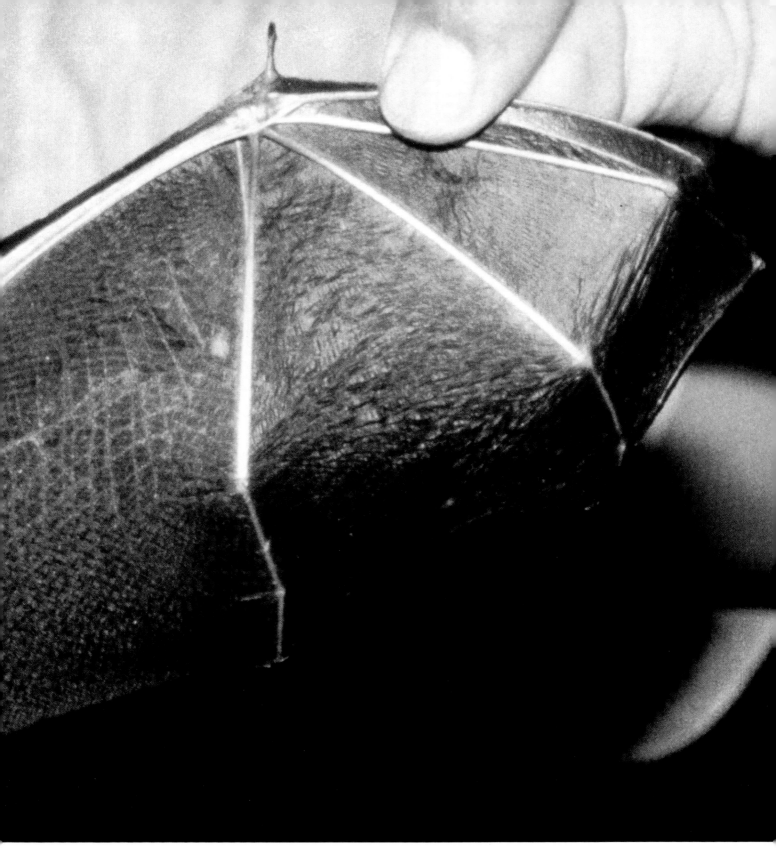

This looks a lot like a wing. But is there a mammal that can fly? ▶

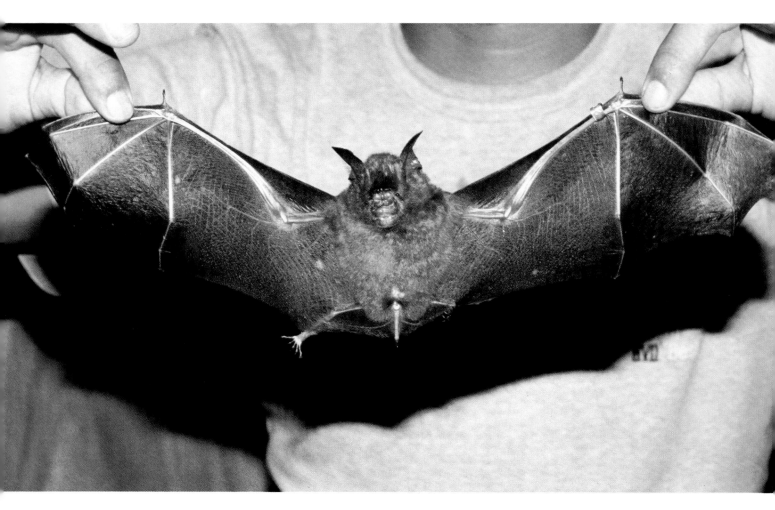

BAT

Bats are the only mammals that can fly. Bats fly on wings made of two thin layers of skin. The skin extends out from the sides of the bat's furry body. Like the cloth of an umbrella that is stretched over the spokes, the skin of a bat's wing is supported by the bones of its hands and arms. A bat's hand is made up of four long fingers and one short thumb that can be easily moved. In this photo, the person's thumb is touching the first and second fingers of a leaf-nosed bat. ■

All mammals can move from one place to another—through the water, in the air, or on land. Seals swim with their flippers. Bats fly with their wings. And horses gallop on their hooves. Can you think of how other mammals use their feet, paws, hooves, flippers, or wings?

GLOSSARY

carnivore: a meat-eating animal

cleft hoof: a hoof that is split or divided

dewclaw: a thumb-like toe on a cat or dog's front paw

keratin: a hard substance that fingernails, claws, hooves, and horns are made from

nurse: the process of a mammal feeding her young with milk from her body

palm: the flat inside part of the hand

opposable thumb: a thumb that can move separately from the other fingers on the hand

retractile claws: claws that can be pulled in or hidden

savanna: a grassland area with scattered trees and shrubs

sole: the bottom surface of a foot

webbed: having toes or fingers joined by skin